LOST & FOUND:
The Awakening

By Stephen J. Talley

COPYRIGHT 2019
© STEPHEN TALLEY

Published by TalleyMarks Publishing

◆ ◆ ◆

All rights reserved. No part of this publication may be reproduced, distributed, or transmitted in any form or by any means, including photocopying, recording, or other electronic or mechanical methods, without the prior written permission of the publisher, except in the case of brief quotations embodied in critical reviews and certain other noncommercial uses permitted by copyright law.

This is a work of fiction. Names, characters, businesses, places, events and incidents are either the products of the author's imagination or used in a fictitious manner. Any resemblance to actual persons, living or dead, or actual events is purely coincidental.

IN MEMORY OF...

...both my grandmothers Clarice Talley and Goldeen Bell;
my friends that I've lost
Nathanial "Lil Nate" DeWalt,
Calvin "Pimp" Davis,
Herbert "Herb" Mercer; and
a lot more friends and family that have been lost. These are the names that popped straight to my mind. So to all of those that are not written, I gave this book my all because of the love and experience that I was fortunate enough to have with y'all! Thank you and I love you!!!

SYNOPSIS

As a reader, you will experience my awakening in the moment of the *awakening*. You will feel my pain, see my horror, and envision the times in your own lives that mimic my own troubling moments. Then you will feel us elevate throughout my journey, and you will gain understanding from your own life experiences.

I will show you my personal relationship and the workings of energy within them all. The relationships are with women that I shared bonds with, my parents, my siblings, my friends, family, enemies, and people I don't know at all.

You will get my truth without a filter. It's my heart, mind, and soul delivered through ink and paper. I will breakdown love, heartbreak, friendships, competition, hate and explain the importance of self-love. Giving you my truth to help elevate your own understanding of the workings of energy and the importance of attaining overstanding of knowledge.

I truly believe I have been given these qualities, to reproduce an exact fabric in mass quantities in finding the next level of understanding within someone else that needed a foundation. I will explain the importance of establishing a relationship with source. *Source* as in the Alpha & Omega, the energy of infinite amounts. The moment of singularity that became two, and then three. The source is in us all, but we are not *Source* individually, but as many, we all equal up to *one*, the greatest masculine and feminine level of consciousness; the balance of both and its importance.

- You enter this book with an open mind, and you will without a doubt find, or should I say, feel as if you are the protagonist and antagonist at some point along *your* way. This book isn't about just who I am; this book is about who *we* are and finding ourselves through the understanding of my experiences, Enjoy...

TABLE OF CONTENTS

Foreword: The Awakening

1. Lost and Found (poem)
2. The Kingless Prince
3. Resentment
4. Finding
5. Exceed the Limit of Greatness
6. Jesus
7. What the Heart Wants
8. Life: Positive and Negative
9. Money
10. Do It for You
11. Delete the Enemy
12. Home (True Love)
13. Purpose
14. The Dream vs. the Agenda
15. The Mask I See Through/The Enchantress
16. Untitled (poem)
17. Knowledge You Possess
18. I'm the Problem
19. The Love from a Father to a Daughter
20. The Woman I'm Scared to Love
21. The Reason I Can't (poem)
22. Family (Lack of Glue)
23. The Man that Remains a Boy
24. The Fire! The Moment it Reignited, the Manifestation
25. The Love Between Friends

26. Crazy In Love
27. Ego and Pride
28. The Trap was Freedom
29. The Know Truth
30. Forgiveness
About the Author

THE AWAKENING

A Foreword from the Author

(It was March 13, 2019 at 8:51am when it all came to me. While texting my daughter's mother, I was struck with an understanding of all the knowledge I had attained throughout my life. The moment was so great that it also put all my experiences of my life in perspective. With this new outlook, I was able to assess this knowledge with a newfound appreciation.)

When they say be careful where you put your love, it's because it's a warning that love is a massive energy force. To love anything is exhausting. Only when you receive the love back will it sustain the energy and release a euphoric feeling that sex and drugs also release. In addition, serotonin is released. Then it becomes an addiction, and you seek that person that's able to give and receive sacrifices of energy and the satisfaction of replenishing it from; which is the high, the replenishing of the sacrifice.

This brings me to why the effect of heartbreak is so exhausting and devastating. You are making a sacrifice of the already exhausting transfer of the energy that is pure positive energy in massive amounts. And you do

it over and over and over until you are completely depleted of energy. You have nothing but an empty space. You have given all of your divine life force away. That energy goes into them and makes them powerful, and it also backfires, but we will get to that later. Now with none of the pure powerful energy of positivity, which comes from the fifth dimension and is that of *Source*, you're left unguarded for the darkness to fill that space that's completed depleted and fights it away. It's why they say if you're filled with light, the darkness can't come in. That's when the hatred manifests; and depression, jealousy, and pain all comes from not
letting go.

You replenish the light in your life and start to push the darkness out when you give all the love to yourself. You fill yourself up with the light and become even more divine than you were before. Meanwhile, the person that stole your divine energy will likely become highly unstable causing them to search for ways to sustain that high like drugs, lust, and spending money abundantly all in desperation of the energy that was stolen. Wow! It's so clear.

So let me continue... The person they're with will suffer because they will never meet the source of energy that they are addicted to; not because they're not bouncing the energy back, but because the energy they are bouncing back is nowhere close to the massive amounts that was given during the heist from the person they left depleted. That person is now beginning to center themselves and becoming one with *Source* at a level far beyond where they were before being robbed.

They have learned to control it because they are in a state of atonement *(at one ment)* with the source of infinite energy that is pure positivity. *Source* teaches you to control your energy instead of flooding you with massive amounts of overwhelming surges of energy. *Source* gradually gives you the energy, and that's why people say that it just takes time not even realizing what they are saying means or how true it is.

People cause setbacks because that thief will take those surges of energy from you but constantly reject you and leaving you depleted which most do. So you start all over and they remain full of energy, but when you stop, they get lost and miserable and you start to glow with a light so bright and intoxicating and controlled and in tuned with source at a level of humbleness so great, you become like a magnet of all light. Your an addictive person to be around because people want to feed off the overwhelming intoxicating glow of your pure positive light. You're ascending to a new level of understanding and becoming enlightened beyond the understanding of even your own reasoning. And it's a controlled light you subconsciously give bits of love out to the ones you love, knowing the damage of your massive amount of energy could do to them. So you in a sense become *Source* and have to learn to control as they absorb and are able to bounce the massive amount that you give at the same force and magnitude of you.

Meanwhile, the thief's world is becoming hell on earth, and out of desperation they do things that make no sense. They take that new partner through hell because now they are both completely depleted of energy; all because the thief's karma is just physics and now the law of attraction is that depleted thief. This is why when dudes come home they're like, "She always come back." Anyway, that thief, out of pure desperation of love, sees their old partner glowing, energy so vast, great, and controlled; they come back hoping to be fed, like a vampire deprived of blood. Like a leach, they are searching for that surge of divine pure positive energy because at this point there life is now full of pain, darkness, loneliness, sadness, anger, jealousy, doubt, insecurities, and hatred. And the once broken is now divine and has the choice to take a risk on feeding them the energy gradually and teaching them to control the slow replenishing of the depleted soul; the soul that is now the embodiment of hell on Earth.

So love is what the Bible says it is; it is the greatest gift of man. It is the greatest a person can give to another because it is a sacrifice of one's divinity and stability of their connection with *Source*. You are at your greatest alone, but when you find your twin flame in which you create a controllable enormous amount of radiant pure positive divine energy, the two of you become one with such unimaginable power in unity. It's as if *Source* created the union himself, and you both have come directly from the same infinite consciousness which is your higher being. It sends out multiple consciousnesses like a pyramid scheme because our whole purpose is so that *Source* can experience life in the form of many. That's why in the times of the beginning of the *Source* there were such divine entities. The closer you get up the pyramid, the closer you get to Source; therefore, the more powerful you were.

Wow! I just explained what the pyramids in Egypt symbolize, Jasmine. And that's why they had the gold cap on the top; the great shining pure light of *Source*. Oh my God, Jasmine, no one has ever said that!

LOST AND FOUND

You still trying to get past the last me but this last me still standing, still coated in gold over the fireplace with a smile on his face

I'm three, four, five niggas past place

And in that race, finished first through last place

No competition, only competing with who I was yesterday

Tried to show you how to be great

When you showed up, now greatness is way beyond your mind state

You still stuck in trying to impress an audience with materialistic bullshit

If you need to be reminded of a boss, I'll pull up real quick

Remind you by showing you that in six months, I surpassed you and yo' bitch

My focus was never about me, it was carrying myself proper-like to represent our family

Your vision was starting to catch beams of light

Now you seem to only exist in the dusk and glow of the moon

at night

    I spend all day bouncing energy back and forth with the sun

    I've reached a level that enlightens the company of your type

    Those trapped in the diminished shines of moon light

    I often try to show you the difference

    You so stuck in pain, hurt, and stressed

    Your vibrations yell out loudly for a rhythm to exist… beyond this darkness

    You see me in your vivid thought, my light still attached to your dreams

    Even through the darkness of sleep my light can be seen

    The brilliant radiant beams that pierce through darkness like a knife to hot butter

    Remember who taught you that you are worthy of being treated as a Queen

    You jumped off your throne to become what a lost individual without any light to be seen

    My light was created within the depths of my soul

    I'm still King and now a King that understands, a King that gives his golden mind to those billions of broken souls

    Your crown sits in the chair that would have always been yours, no woman would have taken that spot from you, but now it's just open air

    A crown with no crown to rest upon

    No hand for me to grab for support

    You broke your own heart believing in the hood

rumor report

    You know all the shit you have done

    Disloyal, disrespectful, feeble immature brainwaves

    Your mind is the equivalent to a pond that has only a ripple

    My mind is all five oceans unlimited and undying infinite waves that's like a thousand times and a triple

    My soul is the equivalent of all seven lands able to reach any and all terrain

    My heart is the sun, and gives life to all up under radiant power of understanding, the purpose of each beam

    Growth

THE KINGLESS PRINCE

I grew up in a neighborhood that was very tight-knitted with us all feeling like family. I have friends that I gained that are still my friends, well they're my brothers. We all share a story very similar when it comes to the household that we were raised in. Only one out of four of us while we grew up had our father in our home. Myself and the other two didn't even truly know if our pops ever even existed. This story I'm telling you is the reality of so many homes of young black men. Boys are expected to grow into men without the stern, dedicated, hard nose love of a father.

It's not broken, no, that's a factor that has absolutely no importance. The presence of the father is one thousand times more important. Understand that a home filled with abuse of any kind from either parent towards the other is maybe even more unhealthy than either of the two parents abandoning their home and family. The energy of the home is one that is filled with insecure, stress-filled tension. This lack of pure positive energy drains not only the parents, but also the children.

The prince that grows up never even knowing that he has a father will one day search for that man. I did and I was twelve-years-old. I was first introduced to my granny. Wow, is all I can say when it comes to the magnitude of love this woman had for me. The complete and total joy and happiness that filled the room is a moment that I will never forget. She was the second person that I had ever met from that side of my family. The first was my pop's twin brother. *Yea, I know right?* And I knew him my whole entire life. Would later be told by my father that my uncle told him there wasn't any denying me. The power of the guilty! By that time I had already forgiven him.

After meeting my granny, I felt so much pure love. At this time of my life I was very, very serious about my grades and maintaining my grades no lower than a B. I was also class president now the second year in a row. I was totally dedicated to sports as well. Well, I'm still very smart and deeply in love with my infatuation to learn, respect, dissect to make my own theories and understanding of the things most in this world accept. I am also a very big sports fanatic. So I feel as if my life is great. I also now realize that even at that age I was absolutely a lady's man; always feeling the need to have multiple women. I now understand that struggle within me.

So one evening while visiting my grandmother, we were walking into her house through the side door which goes into the kitchen, but you can see straight into the den. I immediately knew who the man was sitting on the couch underneath the front side of the house window facing the kitchen. He was flipping through the newspaper. I understand now that he also had the same surge of vibrations and was overwhelmed by things that before were just thoughts but now had become the biggest slap to the face ever in reality. Now as I reflect upon this moment in my life, I understand how powerful of a force I was.

I'll never forget the first thing he said to me. "Do you know who I am?" That came after he said he had spoken to his mother. I responded bold and full of confidence. "Yeah, you my daddy!" No anger, no hate, no resentment. No, not one little piece of it anywhere in me. He asked me, "How you know that?" I'm like, "You look just like me!" So to fast forward the story because this was summer of '98 when I met him, actually going into fall; the first moment I start to feel resentment and betrayal from this man is when I found out that he had a whole family with a grown stepdaughter staying with him also. I think to myself, *how could this nigga not even come out south and see me, and he got a whole family out this bitch*? Nigga, you taking care of a goddamn child that ain't even yours. What the fuck going on? Shit, I'm a spoiled child. My mom replaced the need of a pops with my love to always have some dope ass clothes or games or anything materialistic. Not that she is shallow, no, not at all the reason. I now understand her mindset as well. Unconditional love!

Anyway, that deep seeded value to always get what I wanted turned a spoiled boy from the hood into a young man willing to cut any head to get it. I later evolved into a hustler, then I rose into a man that survived and became more than something so simple as a dope dealer. I became an evolved hustler, able to translate my trapping mentality into whatever I chose to be a part of. So back to '98, learning of the new sister and everything else...The hate in me began to grow when I noticed this man didn't value the gift I had given him, me. I came and found you fuck nigga! That was my mindset. Nigga, you fucking owe me. My moms didn't even put your weak ass on child support. The very least you can do is break me off with a little bread. He started digging himself a big black hole in my chest, better known as my heart. Telling me he was coming and never showing up. This nigga quickly showed his value of love. I now understand that as well.

He still had no understanding of what to do with the situation. This nigga thought I was Trey from *Boyz N the Hood*. Wrong, nigga, fuck you think this is? Yeah, my grades were on point and shit but my nigga, couldn't nothing control me. I had been raised by the niggas in the streets, the infatuation of money, and the desire to control it all. The way he put this feeling in me, I was twelve, almost thirteen and I had already done more things sexually with females in and out of my hood than some grown men. No way can you think that I'm some fuck boy, ever. Again these are my thoughts as I turn thirteen, and I had a girlfriend, who would become the first reason that women would be unable to truly be loved by me as life went along.

I experienced what would be the hardest two to three year span I've ever faced. Two months and ten days after my thirteenth birthday, just a week before my eighth grade year started, the Monday following a weekend of school shopping at Harding Mall, with my mamma, granny and baby sister. I'll never forget how much of an ass I acted because my moms wouldn't buy me a Cash Money pendant and necklace. That Sunday I was supposed to get myself ready to go to my granny's house the next morning. I acted a fool until my mamma called my granny and she said, "Just let him stay out there!" It's like she knew what the next day held, and was at peace with it and wouldn't let it be a traumatizing moment for me. My granny had a massive heart attack that Monday morning, August 3, 1999. I felt guilt about not being there for her, for almost fifteen years, and even sometimes now think it wouldn't have mattered in truth; it wasn't something that could be fixed. She basically died instantly. I love that woman so much. I've lived life longer than the amount of time I was given with her. That's life though, huh? Another reason I'm so hard to love.

Maybe three months later my mother was diagnosed with breast cancer. Nothing in my life was right. Nothing. I was so dark of a person at that moment of my life. My pops tried to be a father, but didn't relate. True enough, I loved him and I still do; don't know why but I do. I started to disconnect from the emotion known as love period. Whenever I do feel like I can love, I'm always reminded of the reality of the world. If my pops truly loved me, he would have taught me to love myself and not the things people can do for me.

RESENTMENT

Bitter irritation and having been treated unfairly.

This feeling is so powerful, it handicaps the heart! Opening your heart for the purpose of letting someone else have it or to love someone else could become impossible until that feeling is let go. This feeling is so powerful, so strong, letting it go isn't what you want! All you want is the love of the same person that put you in the state of mind that you are in.

Resentment is the replay of a hurtful situation visualized on repeat in your head. And it's something that doesn't have to only be toward an ex-lover. Yet, another commonplace or type of relationship that resentment is also experienced in is from a child to a parent. The father abandons his children and the children have to deal with this resentment for large portions of their lives. I know because it took me a very long time for me to forgive my own father.

My resentment towards him never existed until I met him. I was so happy to finally meet him when I was twelve. Then, I met his family; a family I never was given. At that moment, I instantly felt as if I wasn't even important enough for him to come find. The feeling cast darkness in my heart and, I gradually became darker and darker and darker. The death of my grandmother that same year caused for the darkness in my heart to devour me. I was filled with so much hurt, sadness, resentment, confusion, guilt, disappointment, and flat-out betrayal! It created insecurities, unstableness, and a stay away from Love! I would self-sabotage any relationship that became too close. Then shortly after the death of my grandmother, my mother was diagnosed with breast cancer, leaving me to grieve without any type of direction.

Dealing with these multiple life changing events caused me to act in an unreasonable and very irrational manner. The resentment was equivalent to a nuclear bomb! Blotting out the sun of my mind, the explosion of that bomb of emotions created an adolescent becoming a teenager that was lost. I went from being an honor roll student, to becoming a student that was barely getting by. Not because of anything less other than me applying myself.

Over time I gradually broke down the walls that surrounded me that were built by me! I began to see my own flaws with clear vision. My first detachment from resentment was my father. I forgave him, and that's when life started to show me how heavy emotional baggage can be. Now to this day my father and I have more of a friendship than a father-son ship, but the relationship is strong and the relationship continues to grow. I no longer give energy to negative ways of thinking for long periods of time. I've never thought about any of this, not in this manner until now.

I was so afraid in my heart to let people have my full love. For my child, Eva, it was all completely eradicated. My love for her is infinite! Our bond was the beginning of my maturity. I began to grow for more than just myself, I started to put money in the right places. I started to care about other people's feelings. I started to really take into consideration the effects of my actions. And all of this spawned from me letting go of resentment. From me letting go of the hurt that my father caused, something that I had no control over and something that can never be changed. I had to let go of guilt, sadness, and complete hurt of my grandmother's death. I also actually realized that while my mother had breast cancer, I was supposed to have made things easier for her, instead I made things harder. And from that understanding, I've become a man. I've learned now what was holding me back was me not accepting those negative things and then moving on from them. You cannot grow as an individual if you refuse to let go of yesterday. Endure your pains and allow yourself to grow. Put more focus on the things that give you joy!

FINDING

There will always be times that the battle between the negative and positive vibes within you are won by the negatives. That is until you find a way to truly outweigh the very thought that sometimes consumes your mind.

Removing yourself from situations sometimes just isn't enough; it's only a delay in the explosion. You have to learn to eliminate the swelling of anger. Self-control is the point of complete and total love for self. The problem is the emotion, *love* is truly unstable. Highly explosive. Very dangerous to play with and should only be ignited if the people involved regard it with the same value.

So many people mistake the feeling of lust and infatuation for love. Sex should never be what brings together or holds together a relationship. The moment that they are away from the other, the feeling will dissolve. Being infatuated is also that of short term effects. The materials, time and attention, this person blesses you with are short-lived.

Love is caring for a person enough to give them part of you even when they won't give back, or don't have the means to give back. You don't intend to be with this person, but the two of you bounce energy between one another, and this state is also known as friendship. True love is a state in which you find the greatest feeling of balance with this person. The feeling isn't found with anyone else. You two have such a balance that there are times when you feel as if you two share the same brainwaves. You feel a feeling of completion. True love is the feeling that you are willing to die or sacrifice yourself for the safety and happiness of this person. Only because the exact feelings are reciprocated. This feeling should be naturally produced. A parent should always feel as if they will without a doubt be willing to sacrifice their life or surrender any amount of money for the safety of their child, as well as displaying belief in the greatest of their child.

These qualities should also exist in a couple that is engaged. The bond should be way past the physical. These individuals will always have a connection; one so deep they don't need words to explain anything to one another. The purpose of being in each other's life is to give support and unconditional love at all times.

The different levels of this emotion are sometimes very tricky. You have to search the feelings of vibrations and rhythm to know someone's true intentions with your love. Be careful believing what comes from someone's lips. Hear the beat of their heart. The vibes of their words when spoken. Your own mother can be the one that wants to see you fail at times. This is because people have lost themselves and only feel a sense of joy when they hurt others to feel power surging through their being. It's sad, but this happens.

No encouragement, no support; only hopes of financial increase and a feeling of entitlement await this person. This will be the only reason any sort of interest is shown. Distance is needed and has to be gained in order for this person to not fall victim to situations. Convert the negative into positive. Overstand some people's reasoning and purpose. Be able to cipher through emotional lash-outs from people and know the difference between hurt and hate, lust and love. Be the bridge from hurt to healed. Be the equalizer, be the balance inside of yourself. Never be quick to let your temper flare.

Remember, self-control is self-love. Love yourself without fear of failure. Without the thought of others doubt. Be yourself at all times. Find true love within self so that you know exactly who you are. Maintain and fight hard for your beliefs. True love starts from the stomach and when the balance is found, you are then ready to express this feeling to the better half of yourself. This will happen because you have become a magnet to that person's soul. They're on the way!

EXCEED THE LIMIT OF GREATNESS!

I have a vision of me being a man that is great. I want the best parts of life on every level. I want to enjoy my life, become so great and my being that I make a difference for generations to come!

I'm not the first to deliver a message, or even the closest to understand all its meanings. What I do understand is that I want to love those too afraid to love themselves by giving them all that I have to give. I want to show them my pain without any fear of judgment or fear of what my true exposed feelings may lead to. I am an open book to those who are willing to be greater than basic and have felt something of greater purpose to go in the direction of which they've always wanted to go.

I have always felt the need to help those that needed help. These truly divine people were born to unite the world, to align the chakras of the greater being that we are within. The manifestation of the being that is way beyond the depths of feeble intelligence! We are all the creation of the same mind, the same that was brought forth through generations way beyond the books that we have knowledge of. This being is such a greatness and power that we have no understanding. And unless we bring ourselves into a focal point of time, knowledge, and seek understanding we will remain without any understanding.

Keys have been left because this knowledge was not left for the blind; it was left for those without fear of night or day! One that understands the magnitude of what that represents. In having and over standing of what my purpose is, I'm of the belief of just trying to open people's eyes! Not that *their* path is wrong, but there is another path, one that feels more at home. A path that you feel in tune with if you only allow yourself to not be fearful of change. Change never comes without discomfort. That discomfort will dissolve, and you will find a greater you if the change is for a greater purpose. You are a lot better when you are true to yourself. Seek those that vibrate on your frequency and teach the ones that are of an open mind and have a greater sense of purpose. Be the tip of your own pyramid, be that of singularity! And from that singularity, create multiple pyramids over and over again.

Be purposeful with every move you make. Teach with action and lead with the purpose of creating a foundation for another individual. Lead with a purpose of gain for everyone but self. In doing so, you will gain a greater love and respect for self! You have been given this purpose for a reason and truthfully, money isn't the objective. The unity of 1 as 7 billion and 7 billion as 1 in unison is the goal.

A great moment can be achieved by anyone, but greatness that exceeds your life within your designated temple is titled something else. It's an adjective used only for those individuals of a magnitude that exceeds normality. This adjective is being one of prestige and nobility. An individual so distinguished that he/she is known as the Chosen *One*. As if hand-picked by the greater consciousness of *SOURCE*! Learn in your inner space and teach in your outer space. Be the chosen one of your individual universe. Seek knowledge and the overstanding of it. Be the representation of forgiveness, integrity, ambition, purpose, and that of the greatest love you have to give!

JESUS

Love, one of the greatest stories in history is in one of the most loved bodies of work ever. A book that is treated with such a high level of respect that it no longer even needs to be read for most individuals to put their whole belief system within it. The Bible, the book that has been tampered with more than the dictionary itself. The greatest love story ever told; the story of Jesus of Nazareth.

This story is the most beautiful story ever told because it's the story of love. Jesus in the story is the embodiment of love. Love from the *Source*. It begins by showing the greatest act of love given to us by the creator: reproduction. It's clear what the story is saying. Mary is impregnated by the most high. We should all know that this part of the story is not only placing importance on the powerful gift of reproduction, it's also showing how direct and powerful that *Source* is with the woman of Earth. A bond that is greater than man can have with *Source* only. Telling from the beginning the woman is the key to a man's purpose.

Throughout the New Testament we are shown all of the things that love faces. Through any and every moment and throughout this testament love is the key.

At times when you think love would not be present, it outshines any and everything. As Jesus performed his miracles, we are told that the love for *Source* is the source from which his powers are established.

Throughout the book he continues to speak this same tune about loving the Father; never mentioning his mother. This is one of the reasons why I look at the Bible with distaste. It degrades the power of a woman, the purpose of a woman, and the love that is unmatched by any. This is proven during the most defining moment, by not one but two women that bear the same name but are two totally different people. They both are shown to be willing to die for their love for the man in which one loves as a husband and teacher, and the other loves as a son and teacher. She helps him to bear the burden of the weight of the world on his back, and having no regard, no fear, or worry of death. The love from the mother and the wife is unmatched.

Jesus' closest friend, even after being told he would deny him three times still did. He was betrayed for money and even though he knew it would happen, still stayed and faced what was to come. In my eyes this is similar to being in love with someone that is only with you for their own selfish agenda of robbing you of your riches. These individuals are usually covered so deeply with darkness and guilt that they self-destruct taking their own lives, symbolically. Negative energy is able to persuade those weak at heart, mind, and spirit; able to misguide them from love in its greatest form. If it's not unconditional then it isn't love at all!

In saying this I come to the greatest act of unconditional love ever shown according to The Bible. Jesus sacrifices his life for his love of mankind. There is no greater act of love than for a man to give his life for another. In doing this act we are set free from sin, but only through love shall we continuously receive this blessing. This is the greatest story of love ever told. The true ascension up the thirty-three vertebra, and to the crown! Love does not exist if it isn't unconditional.

WHAT THE HEART WANTS

Yes, I know I know the heart can at times be fooled, but the truth is, it cannot. Not when you have understanding of vibrations, rhythm, and most importantly, people. You have to understand that sometimes when you think it's your heat leading you, it is not. You are being led by your ego.

A lot of times the inability to accept failure is what keeps an individual believing that the heart won't allow them to leave or let go. The heart is knowing that a person is thinking of you because you feel *it* within your soul. When seeing this individual, you begin to feel an overwhelming amount of joy. Still yearning for this person months after the relationship has ended. Feeling their touch, and smelling their scent when they are nowhere near you. You and this individual only need to talk. You only need to spend a moment with this person, but both have to live in that particular moment. The past does not exist, and the future is yet to be seen. This moment that is forever the next is the point at which you should place your focus of mastery.

I find myself wanting the woman that I now know

more than ever, I loved completely. Let me address her for a second.

I know that my doubt in your love, which should have never existed, caused me to make decisions of a man that was not yet a husband. As your husband, I should've helped you fight the insecurities. Yet, in the moments in which I sensed those traits, I still found myself entertaining other beautiful women. My heart knows that it cannot truly feel at home unless your presence is felt.

Life is a bucket of *why's*, and for a lot of them you will never have an answer. There are things that will not make sense on this conscious plain. So I say to you, love the one that you love without conditions. Be forgiving of the mistakes that you played a part in creating. Be there in your partner's worst moments. Stay away from an individual that seems to be angry every time they see you. This individual loves you so much they can't stand it. They think about you all day. They are tormented every night before bed. You run, but running can cause unnecessary pain to yourself.

Everything we faced was the ultimate test for a couple that feels like they can say, "I do." The heart has to be strong, the mind has to be prepared, and the body needs to be healthy. Stay strong in your belief in that person. Stay positive through all the insensitive times they will create to attempt to destroy the indestructible entity known as love. The more they fight the love you have for them, the further from themselves they will become. Stand firm and be the lighthouse of love they will need once the reality of what love is dawns upon their soul.

LIFE: POSITIVE AND NEGATIVE

The term "sell your soul for money" is a true statement. Money is a man-made God! People, including myself pledge themselves to this god. They die for it, they kill for it, they steal for it, and they will sell their bodies for it, men and women.

Money is such a force of energy, if you pay attention you can literally see the energy with or without it in an individual. You often times know a person financial status based off nothing but the confidence of their body's movements. The vibrations that this energy gives off are not often anything less than arrogance. These people are so secure by the energy of the money alone they are unaware of the energy's true nature.

Energy of the purity of love cannot be bought nor manipulated. The materialistic desires of the dimension are things the flesh desire, solely based on acceptance. These materials will only be quick satisfactions like that of a hit of cocaine. This is why you see so many people that are rich and famous overdose or commit some form of self-inflicted pain. They can't find love; they don't know love. These people have become so separated from love that they self-destruct overwhelmed by darkness, demons, and negative realms of energy. They are trapped in money, their belief and faith in this cloth that weighs only a gram has the weight of buildings. Money will seduce the mind. Yes, it is a necessity, but it can't be the drive of your reason.

There are multitudes of families, couples, even individuals that are working daily and living paycheck to paycheck. Some don't even know where their means to make the next month's rent, the next day's meal or even where they will lay their heads that night. Although at times they too commit terrible acts of killing their temple, these types understand love with a much deeper understanding. These people are so familiar with pain, hate, and anger that they have depended on love and only love their whole lives. These people of the lower and middle class of life are the true key holders of happiness. People from places of the upper middle class and upper class always want to come to the hood. Often people say things like they want to be cool but the truth is polarity. It's the North and South magnetically drawn to each other.

Love is an incredible force and cannot be matched with something with such little value overall. Money is unable to be taken anywhere beyond the last moment you breath in and the last moment you breath out. Love will carry on and even in some cases create such energy of the human being that they never die. Greatness is never measured by the amount of money you made. The true greatness is measured by what you will do with the money. You have to transfer the energy from money into what you want it to be. You can't love through nor can you buy love from anyone and it be that of purity, from the divine *Source*. Love is that which has no price. You have to balance it all out.

MONEY

They say it's the root of evil, but no, the actions of the individuals are not created by the money. The desires are what control the actions of what people will do for money. Money absorbs the energy of each individual that lays their hands and intentions upon it.

People die for this worthless piece of cloth. No one realizes that the ultimate sacrifice that they are committing for this piece of paper is empowering it more and more. The power of money is so massive that it dominates most of the people in the place that I consider my world. Ninety percent of the people that I know or come in contact with in some form or fashion whole being and purpose is dominated by money. Individuals feel as if they are not able to have happiness without the presence of money.

The crazy thing about the American dollar is it actually has no worth in reality. There isn't anything that represents true worth standing behind the US dollar. When you look at the power of the United States, it's not hard to see and understand the hatred from the countries that display that emotion. We are taking from them and then in order to gain understanding and create the support energy, our country creates an enemy that we all can hate together. Stealing our energy through passion is a lot easier to control when it's given extreme unstable manners. It's either great love through loss or great hate through loss. Either way, the common denominator is loss. No matter what it is that we are losing.

You have to maintain balance within to not fall victim. It's one of the most known to man. It's an explainable purpose only, yet all don't have the level of understanding to overstand the knowledge that money has such a controlling effect over the entire world. Think of the amount of deaths that money has caused, which means all of that power of energy transferred into the money. I believe money is and was made with evil intent. Money was given its power by us, but as the people that use the money, we can take the power back. True enough it will be uncomfortable for a moment, but all change is.

Money has no effect on time; money has no effect on anything that is infinite! We are infinite trapped in but a moment. The fact that we didn't wrap ourselves inside of the multiple traps by allowing ourselves to become devoured by materialistic objects that have no true value to life other than spurts of fake happiness is crazy. To place our energy in the proper places, we have to escape the web of lies that trap us into this materialistic mind-state.

We have to take the God out of money. We have to be greater. We have to love a human being, an animal or just nature in a whole more than we do man-made materials! Why you ask? The answer is simple. Because the statement that we stand under is this: we are willing to destroy the balance of the universe to attain things with no true value beyond that of a temporary satisfaction! Killing things the Divine spiral of *Source* created the same way that we found life ourselves will ultimately be the purpose of gallo self-cleansing and eradicating our species from the planet! If the Earth is the heart then we are the cancer. Love things of life with greater value than something as simplistic as money. Value your purpose and regulate the balance! Money is nothing and we control it! Without us giving it power, power will cease to exist! Stand for something greater self! All right...

DO IT FOR YOU!

Do you ever study yourself?

No, I mean really dissect your strengths and weaknesses.

The key to fixing a relationship in which both individuals want to be in always start with pointing your finger at yourself.

Are you one with enough intelligence to identify your own problems? Do you even consider what your partner believes to be a problem? Now I ask that question because a lot of times people within relationships try to fix or change an individual from being themselves. You can teach one another infinite amounts of knowledge, but what must never happen within the relationship is for anyone to be forced to be someone that they truly are not.

If you love that person, then you grow with that person and endure it all with them, but never to the point you have lost your own purpose, dreams, growth, and character development. You are not meant to stop growing to allow your partner to catch up. NO! You continue to break down barriers of your journey. This will motivate your partner or unfortunately cause envy then jealousy and then that person you were willing to give your hand to, will show you gratitude by simply doing all that they possibly can to steal every ounce of confidence, joy, and will continue to climb. Due to their own insecurities and feeling the pressure of being the mate in the inferior position, they lose sight of any and every ounce of energy that you have given to make them feel self-worth.

Their lack of support is one of the first signs, and more importantly the only red flag that you will ever need to see to know that love isn't present within the opposite side of the partnership. You will know well before this point, but due to you truly being in love with this individual, you will try your damndest to overlook this obvious. This individual's love does not match your own. They drain you of your divinity. Be willing to accept your mistakes and learn from them. If you are a partner in the situation, be willing to let that person go or work harder to become a you that attain greater qualities within self.

There are times when the facts of the situation are not that you did anything wrong; this person or you yourself lack the ability to love because at some point you forgot to love yourself first. Letting go of the situation can be to save the person that loves you unconditionally and to stop you from draining them of their happiness. Letting go doesn't mean giving up. It takes a true person of maturity to sacrifice the temptation to drain someone that's willing to give you every drop until they literally have nothing left to give. Owning the facts of your lack of effort and jealousy is the beginning of the many dark emotions that you will have to face and overcome. The hurt and pain that we sometimes dish out is so great that at times it's unfair to even expect or place the pressure for that person to wait for you. That isn't where your focus should be at this point.

Once you realize that everything that you ever wanted in a person you had, learn from it and then let it go. Release the fear, worry, stress, and insecurities of the thoughts of losing that person. Then start putting every little bit of will power and light into yourself. Create such a distance between you and your old way of thinking that you feel absolute disgust for ever being such a weak-minded person. Do not ever forget that person, because even though that person may have qualities that you despise that person is still you. The core of who you are shouldn't change, just your level of maturity, ambition, reasoning, and ability to love with the purity of a child. This all may sound confusing but it will create a greater you and hopefully a greater y'all.

Forgive yourself, forgive them and forgive any and every other issue that you may have with any and everyone. Letting go of your resentments toward those that hurt you is essential to the magnitude of your growth. Become a man that carries the ability to sacrifice his own pride and ego for the greatness of love. Love shines so greatly compared to those two clear traits of low frequency levels when the traits are directed to self and self only. Start on your journey to catch up to anyone but work at a pace that fits you. When you feel that overloading yourself with work to reach goals of higher heights go for it. If you ever start to find yourself becoming dark because of too much work, you know how to slow your role and maintain that balance.

Meanwhile the woman that you love and that loves you with no limits has been paying attention but you have been so wrapped up in your work that you have caused the universe to bring those things that you love beyond that darkness of something that is a desire. The yearning for your mate is so natural that it happens and you have no control of it. When you lose the desire for something and the love still exists, it has a crazy way of becoming present. So in loving yourself and becoming the greatest of your abilities, and forgive, love, and encourage others, and being a person of positivity and direction, you have discovered that you now have everything that you once had but at a level far, far greater than you ever had a vision for. You let go for someone else's happiness and found out you could fly. What you thought was a sacrifice, was actually the key to the greatest discovery you ever discovered.

LOVE FOR SELF!

DELETE THE ENEMY

I've always, always, always had people that didn't like me. It was so funny too because they really thought they knew my life. You know, they always tried to make me feel bad for being smarter than them. For dressing better than them, for having a mom that spoiled me, and for not allowing myself to be filled with negative energy. Even for having HEART! For fucking their bitch, their sister, their momma or whatever female associate they had. They had no idea that my smile and my laugh were the fabric of my being. The threads of my soul.

I faced so many negative hurtful moments. GOODNESS! The amount of hurt I overcame will always tell you the true definition of the man inside this temple. I've lost so many times, but every loss has always elevated me mentally and pushed me past my limits. I have never stopped being the man that is willing to extend my hand to fallen individuals. My enemies have always been defeated because of my ability to never dwell too long on situations that to some changed them forever. I refuse to allow myself to be smothered or scrambled by darkness.

A negative life is that of an individual that plans to remain a miserable, bitter, fake person. See, I'm such a genuine person, such a honest person that I say fuck being sad; I move on! Don't get it twisted; everything isn't easy to walk away from. The best thing to do is forget about it. These are the moments you become your biggest nemesis! Never feed yourself bullshit. Life is so full of terrible, petty, childish moments that adults, well that is only by age, will literally drown themselves in sorrow. These people have no way of letting things go. They are hoarders of pain. They are energy thieves. Your ex lover, if anything like mine, will—once they see your glow, once they feel your vibe—do all they can to take your energy.

Never allow the actions, unless violence is the problem, to change the person that you are. If I made it through all the hate I faced, all the traumatic events, you too would never allow the same scenario to become an issue. Remember who you are and if people don't accept you, or give you opportunities to become great, then disconnect your entire life from them. Anyone that acts like they are your friend but envy you are the ones you really need to watch. They really are the worst enemies because only time and consistent tests reveal them.

At no point in my life have I ever wanted to be any other man. What I have done is fight to surpass the bar I have set. I'm what the true definition of "don't tempt me" is. I give chances to the undeserving, and throughout my life I've always met competition head on. Yea, I've learned physical fights only ignites the never ending battle. If an individual is unaware of the true battle then he is lost. It's always a chess match taking place when it comes to the battle between rivals. A rivalry is only established if the true self doesn't feel truly inferior to the other. Both individuals will have to feel a sense of a threat, of competition, of a worthy challenge! Never underestimate the power of the underdawg. The man that stands alone without the fear of wins and losses is the true man of superior stature.

The heart of a man is not defined by his money or how he acts when in the winning position. The heart of a man is defined by his actions when he is in a losing position. *How does this man react when surrounded by the enemy? How does the man act and treat people when he is at his lowest point?* The man that I am never stops being himself. Through any and every situation, I have always remained true to the man that I am.

Death is inevitable, but stupidity is controllable. Standing on your own beliefs and manhood is always worth fighting a losing battle. Live for the truth of self, and not for the amusement of the audience. So in saying this, I'm always giving truth to people and their status to me. And how I speak to them is never determined by anything but the choices, actions, and the reasoning and purpose behind that individual's everyday life. I define your status based upon your level of consciousness. Kings think like kings and the rest fall in line. Only way to deplete an opponent physically is to kill that individual. So in my life I have depleted opponent after opponent by mentally placing them on my chessboard until they become more of a problem than a purpose. Then I eliminate them without ever sweating! They were defeated long before their execution. They have been depleted of their purpose and drained of their positive energy. Unless someone else hands them a rope, they will self-destruct., and be in the abyss of darkness. Checkmate! They are no longer on any level of competition. They are devoured by anger, hatred, resentment, doubt, worry, and stress. DEFEATED, from within!

Equip yourself with the weapons of greater means. Jewels are given but will you absorb this or will your feeble intelligence level reject it! Always remember that once a man establishes himself as a threat to your manhood and once your foot is on his neck, crush the whole windpipe, metaphorically speaking of course. Destroy the confidence, eliminate the will power, and crush the purpose.

DEPLETE THE ENEMY!

HOME (TRUE LOVE)

The word alone gives you a satisfying feeling of safety and comfort. A man will dedicate who he is to a woman he loves and the kids within the home. The love will be all a dedicated man will ever need to pick up his spirits daily. To have a woman that shares the same visions and dreams as your own is not only a roll of the dice by the universe, but the equivalent of someone hitting the lottery. It's like you only had one try and you actually won. But not even the winner of the lottery can match the moment these two intertwined their energy.

Sometimes these flames of love will clash, just like anything else. They are the exact same but completely opposite; the duality of polarity! These two once in sync, will shine so much brighter than any other relationship within a hundred-mile radius either direction. That to me is how rare the finding of the perfect fit happens. The craziest part of this is, if these flames are separated for long amounts of time then its very possible for wither one to not be willing to come back in contact quickly.

The feeling of being helplessly in love with someone that could possibly have hurt you takes a toll on one's heart, mind, and soul to the point they become ignited. No matter what though, when you're home, you're home. The address may change, but what never changes is the overwhelming feeling of comfort, purpose, safety, and love! You can fight it, you can try to extinguish the flame between you and this individual, destroy the BOND!! Truth is, destroying anything about this individual, is destroying you. You will never again feel at home again while in this specific temple! The children, the job, and the future will always feel as if something/someone is missing. In truth your subconscious mind is taking you on a level deep within the fabric of your being. Your connection to *Source*, the infinite consciousness and level of understanding that knows the beam of light that split and created the twin of your flame that yearns for the connection to be reestablished.

True love doesn't mean that every moment will be perfect. No, TRUE LOVE means that you will be able to overcome any and every obstacle that comes at them. The strength that these two create once together as one being. The greatest part of it is *Source* will be the arms supplier for the battle and war until the point both of them ascend to the next dimension, intertwined in the energy and have perfected the practice of the kundalini. They will travel up the thirty-three vertebrae in sync as if the Indian man with a flute is playing the tune at a frequency of hertz as they rise to, not the fourth, but fifth dimension. No negative energy exists within this dimension. You, the immortal being that you are, have found the purpose of the story of Jesus, and to yet another level and degree.

Thirty-three, the age of Jesus, was the key telling you through the crown is the way. This level can not be reached alone. That is the part that is realized while he carried the cross. Who helped him carry the cross? His wife and mother did. Two women who both have TRUE LOVE for this man. Both only rivaled by one another. Only one energy can be greater, well, of greater magnitude and that is from self. The true love is established with self as the foundation and the house is built with the partner. The true Home is then established.

PURPOSE

It takes a man to admit his wrongs and to let go of his ways and rebuild his life. To know that there are things that outweigh and are worth putting his ego and pride to the side a man will unlock the side of his brain that is thought of and also labeled the feminine side. This side of the brain gives him the ability to connect with emotions. This gives him the ability to think outside of his linear dominated mind. He understands that to become one with himself and to have that in which he seeks, the feeling of completion of success, with the woman that he felt this state with, he has to begin to try to understand this woman on a level that his mind has not been completely open to.

We all have both sides of gender in our DNA. To be like that of the divine means that you have to balance the two. The brain is meant to be made whole and we are to unlock the power. In becoming a man, he loves and knows that the true power of real love is unconditional. No greater sign of love than forgiveness! Having forgiveness for the mistakes made by others that are also on a journey to reach the state that you seek. I've become that man and in becoming the man that I am, I have true and unconditional love.

First, for myself, I am able to endure the hardships of the third dimension. I connect to *Source* and depend on the positive pure energy from which all came, *Source's* eternal love. Second is having enough love to try to help others understand it all. Sometimes they are so deep in hell you have to let it all go to ensure that you do not fall into the pit that hold them captive. They will have to find their own rope of happiness. Third, I've established the state of mind to be able to let go of resentment, hate, and everything else connected to darkness. I am a man, and it takes a man to love a woman correctly so that he is able to lead them as one to Eden and beyond. Raise your vibes and know that being man is more than money, sex, more than it all. It's the combination and balance of it all obtained to reach love on a level that is unable to be understood by boys.

It takes a woman to accept the reality that she just might be the gas to the problem. It takes a woman to focus on trying to lift her man up and always be his number one fan no matter what she may have heard. A woman with real love is one that gives no attention to words from anyone trying to kill the image of her king. The love of a woman is a force without limits of any kind. This woman will go to the ends of the earth to prove to this man that she will be the greatest woman that he will ever need instead of giving focus to any negative entertainment from those that dislike their happiness because of the darkness they sit in. Snakes are everywhere and sometimes you are sleeping with the snake. As a woman, never discredit the efforts of hard work, selflessness, and happiness given by a man.

Most of all, never make a man feel as if his sacrifices don't matter to you.

A woman understands the chain reaction that is created based upon the Divine Purpose, "Cause and Effect." A man needs a woman that unlocks the feminine part of his brain by becoming that part of him. He in return should give her the masculine side of the brain power, so that once in rhythm with balance of energy and both are in sync with the direction in which they will send their energy in unison. They then become that in which a married couple is supposed to be. The transformation from two to one seems to be subtraction, but in reality the fusion of the two creates a bond of three. They then become the Divine, connected to *Source* as one perfectly fused being of purity; the woman replacing the rib back into the man, and bringing the spiritual balance of mind and clarity between the two.

The woman is the key to the man's success. Not the success of earthly objects, but for the purpose of our beings. In my opinion and this is my opinion solely, though with the population being whatever it is at this point of creation, it's almost a guarantee that I share the same thoughts with at least 200, 000 other individuals on this level of reality. I believe that our purpose is based upon this finding ourselves first through experience through pain, happiness, desperation, contentment, love, hate, etc. During this journey, both the man and woman beings are being told to reproduce, reproduce, reproduce! It's an innate desire of the soul to maintain immortality. The soul also understands that the creation of the next being is created by the Divine

Unity rather than that in which God is not involved. Not saying that what is created cannot be attained by the Power of perfection when connected to that individual's twin flame!

THE MASK THAT I SEE THROUGH/THE ENCHANTRESS

The absolute most unexplainable thing is the actions of the guilty. These people will only possess the ability to make themselves feel vindicated in their actions. This individual is a very pathetic person; very rarely taking ownership of anything they do. This hopeless individual is one that will be happy with hearing other's validation of their lies. Such a sad and sick individual.

This person whether man or woman, or should I say boy or girl, has either been mentally destroyed, manipulated by friends or just an extremely self-centered individual. This person wears masks all day and all night. During times of extreme emotional trauma, that is when this person is no longer able to wear masks to cover the true nature of their character. They are usually entangled in so many lies, and emotions they don't even know who they are. These people carry so much weight and so much bitterness and hatred for themselves that they are nothing but what is also considered a black hole. These people are totally lost to the reality that is beyond the world they have created within their own head. They do so to make themselves feel a sense of freedom from the amount of pain they have dished out to other people or should I say victim after victim.

I have no tears for myself, only for those that I deceived when I was full of pain and hatred. Only when I realized that I was the only one ever at fault and forgave myself and I forgive those that hurt me did I realize that I was a man full of a sense of freedom. Releasing myself from the prison of the bullshit lies after lies only then was I able to notice that I'd be lying to myself. I tell myself to always be honest to those that are even worthy to hold a conversation with you. If you take the time out to hold a full conversation with someone, why waste any of those moments of time wearing a mask not being yourself? I just wasted a portion of my life that can never be replaced.

Being honest with myself I now believe this person was introduced to my lifestyle and my status in theses little areas, and so she decided to try to use me to make her ex mad. I care not about any of the things that are just pure speculation. There is absolutely no truth in my claims because there are no facts to support it. This woman is very unstable. The masks that she wears are of that of a woman of light problem; she absorbs even the mask of the woman she once was. The most horrific part of this woman is she has problem with being grateful. She has a problem with the truth and she immediately becomes uneasy, defensive, and runs. She will do all that she can to rid herself of the demons and make up multiple scenarios to escape facing the truth. She then becomes the "Life-long Victim" aka the Enchantress.

She starts first provoking you to strike her. Even if you don't physically hurt her or verbally abuse her, this girl will still immediately go into character. These individuals want you to praise every little thing they do, and I mean everything. I mean in truth they pretty much don't want to play their role to the best of their abilities but expect you to go above and beyond that of just average. Guess what you do? You replace their mask and maskless face that was once yours and used to be filled with a sense of extreme joy. Your joy is sucked right into that abyss of coldness. In fact, you begged for this woman. You left your home, your 10-month old baby. You started fucking this girl when your daughter was only two months. This was sign number one of this woman's unstable mind.

Red flag number two: the actions she displayed due to her hurt feelings, not to mention you fucking the life out of her on the first day you met her. She fucked your enemy and homeboy to spite her ex. She even gave you this man's Playstation out of pure spite. Red flag number three: The want for attention. How can someone with absolutely nothing but the weight of her life ever act as if you don't deserve her without the mask at all times? The effort alone of this man to raise not one, not two, but three kids who are not his own child wasn't enough to deserve it? Not to mention helping you to heal all of your hurt. But you disrespected this man because of his kind heart to you. You took his love for granted. You wore a mask covering your true self all the way up to the point when the police kicked the door in two days before the wedding.

While this man is behind bars you grind your ass off to get the bond money. You go hard for nine days and from the money he had in the streets to the weight of his name you are able to come up with $9500 at one jail and $2500 at the other jail. Thirteen thousand all off the weight of this man's name. This is the type of man you were dealing with but as soon as he comes home you showed him just nine short days you already were unable to be trusted. Nine days and you had already let another nigga in your head. You already chilled with this man's closest friends at that time. The only thing in your mind should've been to use that nigga for your nigga to get out but then expose that nigga for the fuck shit he was on. If you choose to lie then that is because you were already feeling guilty for things you had done. Your disloyalty came based off the words of another man. This means the amount of love in this woman was already dead.

This woman may have at some point wanted to be a wife, but if the insecurities within a relationship are so great that you become completely engulfed in trying to prove that this individual is a bad person you in actuality may just be creating that which you fear. Any woman that allows another man that's supposed to be her fiancé's friend to say anything to damage that man's character and hang on to that other man's every word is in all actuality weak-minded. I created this chain of events though. I was the one who started the whole chain of events. No, I was the one who was at fault. Without any doubt in my mind, I know I was.

The first time I got the feeling and I was over the bitch, I let her right back in. I hurt a woman that never wore a mask and still never wears one. I have nothing to fix with her; only shit that I destroyed. At this point of my life there are no masks that will fit anymore. Truth is all I have to give you. I won't waste a breath telling anything less than the truth. Lies are something I'm finally freed of. No guilt, no lies, no lines I'm not supposed to cross. I'm freed from all my bondages. There is no better way to clean up the lies once you start telling them. You eventually start to become addicted to it. You no longer care; you just want to see how you can get away with them. That mask is also very taxing to the soul. You will eventually be the reason for you own broken heart.

The key to happiness within a relationship is both people working in unison in love, confidence, trust, honesty, loyalty, integrity, and respect. If you intend on finding happiness within yourself or in anyone else, you will need to lose the mask which eliminates the darkness of deceit, guilt, and disloyalty.

THE DREAM VS. THE AGENDA

Something like this is realized further into the relationship. The individual that is into it for the purpose of gaining a leg-up is the one with an agenda. This person is usually an energy thief. Time and love never appreciated. Go way beyond the fact of if that person truly cares for their partner. This problem was created sometimes many years before these two individuals ever knew of the existence of one another. What is very unfortunate is the energy that drives a dream in infinite amounts if the individual has put their whole being into the fantasy! A very truly horrible heart-wrenching manner!

For the previous chapter, the life-long victim, the enchantress, is the role of this individual. The man in the sand is willing to believe that she will change by giving her multiple opportunities to leave the situation. This man puts the whole world on his shoulders, makes life everything she never had and got into the belief she was undeserving of having. She feels that she can only attain the things that she wants by getting them herself or for her children. This has taken her agenda away from her, for the moment!

The moments, no matter how many, do not hold lasting effects. Sometimes within the moment the vicious black widow within this woman rears its ugly face. This man still doesn't let her immature actions deter him from the dream of them having a family and becoming successful together. This is the type of love given unconditionally since the moment they began their first conversation. The situation that seemed to be a moment of magic! The desire for this woman is lust-filled to begin with. When they got together, she quickly but without any aggression applied her will and cast this man up under a spell. From the first encounter into the moment this man is completely drained of all abilities to function.

The dream and this is a very horrible truth of reality, that both clearly realize it's a dream that won't fucking die because of the faith love, and greatness of a dream! To kill the one who plays their Divinity within the belief has to shroud the thought with negative energies to keep them from developing faith in the resurrection of the once prominent and immaculate relationship. This dream was like a star, and they grew bright just like the cycle of a star. The problem with this star is that it had no longevity of stability. The effects of the star shake the universe from just major arguments. It seems as if every time something very devastating happened to remind them of their importance to one another.

Now after the destruction of the star that was once their immaculate dream, there is only a black hole is left! The controlling party which has always been the one fighting to keep hold of any light is the enchantress. She has devoured the dream, and sucked every piece of energy out of the star that skate instant vacuum of energy that was created from the implosion; they created the enormous explosion love between the two individuals!

Although I did state that all energy was sucked into the vacuum, as I write I realize, I am incorrect! Large amounts of the energy remain, but the remains are not as one; they are broken into shards that are scattered. The dream still lives! The dream cannot be devoured by the darkness of the misled heart of the agenda. Each shred of energy is hope that it will be given the opportunity to piece itself together with old energies and new ones that become available with time.

This energy wants to shine so bright that it becomes an assassin of the feared and thought to be an undefeated black hole. Slowly the agenda doing those without light to feed itself. The woman devours countless stars before realizing the truth of her failure, of her loneliness, her inability to sustain happiness, and her greatest, greatest issue which is trust! It is within her to destroy the darkness within herself. Each star she devours increases the size of her unfulfilled heart. She has to stop the vacuum! The resentment that creates this massive amount of hatred is deep seeded! She is lost, and she's lost because in order to protect her feelings she chooses to be a hate-driven individual. This will only end with the destruction of herself!

Happiness and long-lasting joy will always leave her quickly because she kills all light! She needs to find love within herself! The dream will begin to re-establish his light, and once again formulate a dream no longer hindered by a force he never knew existed. The dream and the agenda, the yin and the yang. I say that to say this, balance can be found with perfection when dealing with the situation. The dreamer is a wizard with infinite powers that can also break the woman from the cage of darkness that she has created. She can begin to forgive the world so that she finds balance within herself. Now, overstand me correctly! I stated he can break her out; it's up to the powerful Enchantress to allow herself to ascend from the darkness she has been so deeply rooted within.

The wizard or the dreamer doesn't have to perform magic of deceit. She will only need to be shown that the dream can become a reality with love! Manifesting reality out of the dream makes the thread that once held them together now strong rope! With every step the dream becoming reality and that man enduring the hardships of that woman, their bond grows stronger! The enchantress's agenda is no longer that of a narcissist! No! She believes, and grows into something so bright and beautiful it is as if the woman is pregnant! The glow is of the same source that creates the glow of a woman that is impregnated. This woman is realizing the power of loving self and the greatness of forgiveness and trust which is needed in love. This glow is no longer being tainted with hatred. This glow is the birth of this woman's Divinity being restored!

Now these two are no longer the star versus the black hole. These two have become one, and now as one they are a universe of their own! The agenda is the dream, and the dream is the agenda...Balance is found, perfection is realized, and now the time has no digits!

Love has no limit if love is never given up on!

UNTITLED POEM

Compare me to who?

Stop it, my understanding alone breaks the banks

What you get a watch or some bricks

Lol, but I'm the one that show the whole iceberg of love

With anyone else you scared to move off the tip

Always had you on my hip

You were always there when the cameraman was about to shoot

Brough off my hip and will kill shit

No matched, never matched

The truth of the love will be the same reason why our fingers interlock

Within the pure ecstasy of our flames reconnecting and me entering into your womb

The moment in which we will once again feel free

A real oxymoron, huh?

The cage that we have both been

Locked in individually, can only be

STEPHEN TALLEY

Unlocked by us becoming one again

Yeah it sounds like total bullshit

But tell me what happens when you give me something as simple as a kiss

Something as basic as a hug

The vibrations of our presence around each other are powerful

The uneasiness, it's so clear

You use your defense mechanisms

And sadly yours are that of creating more distance

You think you are greater

But you stepped down from your throne

You stepped down from love

You fight the better half of you

We will become one and you feel it

I'm still here, not dead, not hurt but you filled with more power than ever before

You fill me with your truth; it's laced around your words

It's okay, I accept them both

I've let go. I no longer push or pull

I allow the power of the divine to do what they want

Love, do as you see fit.

I'm the only one of this mind state could understate

I've ascended from boy to man from man to grown man

To a grown man at one with *Source*, I'm a divine being

My heart, I think is one of the most crazy parts of my being

I always try to help bring them to the light of truth

I have to realize all the things that I warned her of

They not here for me

They are of the greed beam

The hate beam

The anger beam

KNOWLEDGE YOU POSSESS

Too many times I've held on tight when I should've just let something go. It's my gift and my curse. I'm a man full of optimism and persistence. This attitude is beautiful, but you have to know within yourself when it's time to let go. Put your best effort in but do not allow yourself to become lost in the want for anything. The universe feels your vibrations and will shape the reality of your true beliefs. Be mindful of your beliefs.

So the greatest quality a person can have is love. Forgiving someone shows so much love to that person, and more importantly to yourself. Being the type to hold on to grudges, resentment, and guilt you are the type that will never have happiness. You can't find balance holding on to things that only take energy from you. Now in saying that, I don't mean that being an optimistic individual is bad. What I'm saying is do not give all of your energy at any point to things that only absorb it. You see athletes dedicate all of their energy to become a pro athlete. The payoff and energy balance comes from practice. Seeing your skills elevate and with every praise of your skill your energy rises. Confidence which is the love for yourself in specific areas rises.

Being the best at your abilities at anything requires confidence. Even in the case of relationships. The only thing is you have to have confidence in another being which equates to trust. Trust is the confidence in someone else and you only give trust to those you love. That's exactly why people have to earn trust. I hear people all the time say they love everyone. I think to myself, *then you are the one that will face a lot of disappointment.*

You have to be realistic while in a dimension filled with beings filled with dark energy that they don't know how to escape because they are not even aware of the state they are in. They need guidance and the truth is we all do. No human being is greater of a being; only one of greater understanding and knowledge. No matter the level of status, there will always be energy of equal ability. The strength is finding the balance between the two, so that you are able to raise your level of positive pure energy and not be attacked by negative energy too great to fight against. This is why the balance of the energy is essential for a being throughout one's lifetime inside their temple while in the third dimension of darkness. You have to fight to become strong enough to understand the state of existence you are in. This dimension is one that will remain on repeat until you break through the mirage of this life being it.

We are beings of immortality; we never die, ever. We are like everything else within the energy of all/

Source/God. Nothing ever ceases to exist; only transforms into some other form of existence. An example of this is water. Water is immortal, complete of divinity. The combination of two hydrogen atoms and one atom of oxygen is a living organism. Water is all around us. Water is a dominating factor of life. Water is key to life in the understanding of humankind. I'm not one to speak upon life of all because my understanding of life is limited even upon this earth. If polarity is true in all of existence, then maybe there are organisms that can only live with the absence of water. There may be things in existence that are not within the realms of our understanding. The materialistic things of this dimension have been designed to blind us all from the want and need of knowledge and understanding of all that we learn. It's why so many find themselves submerged in and devoured by subjects and matters without much substance.

In saying all of this, I'm basically saying you can only understand or begin to try to understand that of which the knowledge you possess.

I'M THE PROBLEM

Throughout my life I've always been my greatest critic. Instead of blaming anyone for the shit I went through, the true fault never went any further than me. It has always been my choice to do whatever led to the events that took place, no matter if they turned out good or bad. It's always been up to me! I've been the one to destroy me; even in this last relationship. Instead of killing my old habits, I allowed my drug habit and darkened soul to completely destroy my greatest quality. I hurt the woman that I loved. Who knows though; the universe puts the pieces in place based on vibrations of my heart. My true mind manifests the reality of truth. The truth is I asked for all the bullshit to be removed and the truth of Kayla's actions and true feeling be revealed to me. Then BOOM! I'm shown. Then I forget immediately of the request I asked and prayed for. Here it is, fully exposed. Maybe these things are all due to me manifesting them. So instead of defeating myself, and being devoted to anything but my greatness, in turn I overlooked the love being given.

Never regret the decisions that you made, no matter where it took you. Own that shit and become greater than the "weakling" that made those bad choices.

Greatness is realized when you grasp in your understanding the moves needed to be made in order to reach that level of physical and mental state. Give your body the respect that it needs to support your brain to process thoughts appropriately, lungs to inspire and expire air, heart proper nutritional value, and cleanse your body of toxic things you love so much, which in this case, drugs!

Let the drugs go! Release your pleasure locks with the keys of success. Dominate the world! Dominate the man in the mirror. Who is he? Who am I? I'm the man in search of truth, knowledge, and the mental power to understand. I am the man that will die for his family. I am the man who lost love for himself trying to prove his love to a woman. I am the man that cheated and cheated anytime he wanted. I am the man that feared the loss of his loved ones. I'm the man that knows he has problems with drugs.

I am the man, I am the man!

Now I will be the man that takes his message farther than the notebook paper it's written on. I'm asking for guidance to escape the moment of no knowledge to write to those in need of it. One with all! We are of amazing amounts of light and perfection of *Source*, such that we have the same abilities; we just have to unlock them. Remember what you've already learned. I've been looking ahead but maybe the balance will rise even more when I learn to also look into the past times back before I was in this specific temple. Was I even Black? Was I one with wealth and have come every single time as that of poor descent? My heart tells me that I will be one of wealth. I remain in that mindset.

I won't allow myself to lose.

Eva, you will have a father present in your life. You are of a man that won't let you down. Give me the greatest opportunity and I will make good on the message of the true Creator. I will devote my energy enlightening all of those that are lost. I will create summer camps and homes for those less fortunate. Give me this opportunity! Guide and protect me. Darkness is everywhere. Let me be one filled with light so bright that I brighten the minds of all those that even gaze upon me. I won't fail. Life is all about giving all you can to gain, understand your existence, reproduce, enjoy and ascend.

THE LOVE FROM A FATHER TO A DAUGHTER

The moment when you finally hear that you have a baby on the way, you want it to be a boy bad, and BOOM...you're having a girl. From that point I knew. Back then I didn't understand, but I do now. I became afraid because at the time I didn't have anything together. I was over 100 miles away from her and I still felt as if I was suffocating in the worry of not knowing how. Then just like that you were coming out.

I'll never forget the energy that came out with you. It was so clear to me what I had to do. I had to protect, cherish, and provide for that beautiful beam of light. Our attraction was not one that wasted time happening. I now understand what that was. You are me and that part of me that you are is the greatest part. Our pure energy was mending, combining, and establishing an unbreakable bond. At the moment when I held you, the *Source* of all was bright. The pure love was undeniable. My Eva, my soul, my eyes! You were the love of my life. Everyday I fill my life with you, but in doing so start to become distant from your mother. Not because lack of love but me not wanting to let you down. I work hard and I climb. I walk away from family not because of lack of love. No! My heart finds more balance with this other woman. I never lost you in the equation. What I did do is hurt a beautiful spirit. In doing so, I hurt you too. I would pay dearly for the next three years, then find myself totally paralyzed a year almost two after that.

Our bond never weakens but gains strength while we mix with another family and your mother creates and additional piece to hers. We experienced some very tough heart wrenching times, never having to be apart, but facing it. You with all your love carried me on your little back. We both cried the times we got to see one another and we cried on the phone when we spoke to one another. Our love for one grew intense and then came for us to reunite. I remember it like this...

It's 8:31am on December 6, 2018 and I hear a car pull up outside. I can feel your vibrations of love before I even opened the door. The feeling of us reuniting is that same feeling we had when I held you April 16, 2014. The energy of pure positive love. You balance my soul. Through my dark times after being released you wiped my tears. You told me it will be okay, you loved me as if I were your child. Again carrying your father's spirit and cleansing it with such purity that the darkness I was in washed away whenever you were here. You and I get over the hurt of betrayal together. No one cared how we felt, no one but the ones who were always there. Your granny, aunts, your MOTHER. The love she gave us was that of a true friend for me and that of a lioness for you.

This is the moment we are at now: you're almost five-years-old and we have experienced quite a bit. The most major part though is you and I never abandoned each other. You and I grew even closer. I'm your superhero, and you're my guardian angel. No love is greater than that of a parent and a child. How can men miss out on these types of feelings?

As long as I'm breathing, no matter if I'm broke, rich or average, my love will forever be of an infinite magnitude and directly from my divinity when it comes to her. My brightest light on earth, isn't the sun, moon, or cameras, it's my second coming, my Eva.

Dedicated to my greatest gift to the world, the greatest gift given to me from *Source*. Daddy loves you for as long as you can close your eyes and see, I'll always be right there. We are one living through two. I love you. Be great. I look forward to writing more about us in five more years.

Love,

Super Dad

THE WOMAN I'M SCARED TO LOVE

There is a woman in my life that I love so much that I won't allow myself to be with her to hurt again. Not yet. I won't be with this woman without being completely dedicated to the love that she deserves. We are great friends, and respect each other. She gets to love me without fear of being cheated on. I'm not a good man to love at this point. But I will win. Fuck these pills; fuck the life of that of a failure.

So many people fail because they lose themselves chasing after the wrong things. Having this woman to give me direction and for me to also give that same effort back to means a lot. Our child feels a lot of happiness, but disappointment still lingers from the loss of our family. I refuse to let her be a part of another unhealthy family environment. She will never have to feel abandoned or forgotten. No bitch will ever get close enough to my child to hurt her because my bad choices in women. Maybe I'm the creator of these bad women. My unstable ways have somehow created the insecurities in the woman to take over knowing my history, and more importantly our history creates an impossibility of us ever being together.

The resentment is still there. The level of pain that I caused someone that I love and will always love. It is a reality that I hate to face, but it is a reality that I have no choice but to accept. Showing you my greatest love is me accepting the fact that you and I will no longer be able to have a contact on the level that includes feelings. Your love for me is so great that you don't respect my love for you at all because I hurt you. The pain, or should I say resentment within you takes your sight away when it comes to my love. No amount of apologies, no amount of love, gifts, or anything will erase the pain I caused. I proposed to another woman in front of the whole world, including you. Something that you thought would be us.

I truly cannot love you whole-heartedly because you will try to hurt my soul. You won't be able to help yourself. You will eventually use my greatest love on any level of life; the life that is the perfection of me. You will take her from me; you will make it difficult for me to be there at moments that are once in a lifetime moments. I will endure and overcome each and every attempt. I won't be perfect in these moments, but I will be great. I will face times in which I will again put my ego to the furthermost parts of my mind. I will not fail as a father. I will be the man she needs despite the hardships you and I will face.

I am scared to love you because of these future events that are certain to take place. The craziest part after all our arguments, after all the pain that we will inflict upon one another, I'll still die for the life of the mother of my child. I'll still love you. I'll still support your dreams. I'll still pick you up when you fall. I'll still attempt to be more than just a co-parent with you. I'll still be your friend. We will see what happens, but life proves to me daily you will become one of my greatest friends over the span of our lifetime. You just won't be the woman that will be mine. I love you, no matter what, I love you; it just scares me to know what it has come to.

THE REASONS I CAN'T

Beautiful, you are that and more than I could ever put into words

The way you love unconditionally is the same reason I haven't

It's the same reason I can't

You will not be

Cause I will not let you be

You are the greatest woman that I've had in my life and I really don't ever want to ruin that

I have shit to fix, I need to be better

No way will you be a rebound to anything I just went through I could never allow that

My greatest act of love in my life

The sad part is you probably won't even understand it

You don't deserve a relationship of me not focused on just you

Not saying there's other women but saying you're not at the forefront of my focus

Yes, I'll provide all I can but the caliber of relationship

you deserve will only hinder our focus

You still hang on to resentment. My fault, it happened, but your job is to let it go

We could never truly be happy if that's something you refuse to let go of

My friend, you are because my friend is the best thing you can be

This doesn't mean I don't love you

It just means I can't give you the best of me

I am restricted because I'm still putting the pieces back together: Me

I can't lie to you about anything

I'm doing all I can to be better

Strength is gained and then loss

But not to that ungrateful girl

I lose strength because the fight within myself sometimes become so exhausting against the negatives

I won't lose and I fight for my gravity

I am happy that I'm free from the fake love, but the bitch still has a part of me

I'm prying away the pieces and realize that in order to truly be done, I have to sever the ties completely

I love those kids and that's the part of it that hurts still so deeply

But what the fuck am I hurt for when they've moved on and adapted to the new nigga?

Because the reality almost everyday they hit me up to say they love me

Just the way Mila tells me the same

The shit that this selfish bitch has done is crazy

You are ten times greater a woman outside and a hundred times greater on the inner

But with you I can't allow myself to be a winner

I have to lose this time so that you can win

I can't take anything from you because I don't deserve it

I can't ask you to forgive me or to get over shit

I can't ask you to just forget

I won't. I can't!

I love you forever and ever but my heart agrees with my mind

Being with you right now is something I can't

Thoughts on this poem...

    Writing this poem is a difficult thing. All the pain of this sacrifice, wow! I never understood the magnitude of hurt and resentment I had toward myself. I let my family down. Not for a great enough reason either. Not to protect them, but to be with someone who never deserved shit from me. She never deserved a shred of me. Maybe she loved me, but she was never healed from the last nigga. And here I am in the same position. The irony! She lies and lies and lies some more. I was the joke for leaving a Queen for a hoe. Love, I'm sorry!
Sorry isn't even close to enough...
    I love you!

FAMILY (LACK OF GLUE)

The greatest loss that I took over the past year and a half was hands down the togetherness of my family. To lose the pure love of them together everyday rips at me daily. They're my reason to get up. They are my reason to lie down. The thought of them thinking I didn't do enough is clearly not something that should ever be believed. The woman that I still feel in my chest daily, and sometimes write poetry about and send to anyone only becomes a turn of the page.

She gave up on more than just me, and she can't understand that. The resentment for me is the dark negative energy that she is captured by. She has no idea the magnitude and pain she caused not just to me, but our family as a whole. She can blame all she wants and I'll accept it daily. The problem is she won't truly love herself or anyone else completely until she lets go of all grudges, resentment, guilt, and fear. The mask she wears daily will soon fade. The love for herself will bring upon the awareness of the wrong she has done to someone that loves her more than she will ever be able to understand; that is, until she is able to understand what love is. Until she understands the part she played created that which she fears. One thing can only repair through time and complete dedication and effort. Trust will be given once one of these individuals begins to give the other love without doubt or worry.

The fact that we still argue and she still runs away from truth and reality, and hold on to opinions, lies, and deceit shows how truly regretful and unhappy she is daily.

I forgive you and I know you want to be in my arms. Come on home! Recreate the unity of our family. Leave the darkness, walk right out of it, and complete the light of our twin flame. Without you I'm unable to be complete, and no matter how much you want to fight it, truth is you know it! The truth is you are incomplete too.

~~~~~~~~~~~

What makes family so great, so needed?

People.

The ones that are filled with destructive darkness. I don't need anybody. I look at them, not with pity, but with reason with such a sense of hurt. You never truly experience the totality of happiness, joy, or understanding until you have that energy of love within the full circle of family. So much energy, so much pure love. The hate that comes at family is very strong. Sometimes family will feel so broken but the love family possess over time will overpower all darkness. Time will not be a factor. That which is true and of the same beacon which family becomes has an attraction to be together. The universe is a force that hears only that of your true heart's desire. You can fight it, but as long as you fight the happiness that you desire, it will never be truly attained.

The love you desire starts with you and this love when true and pure will work with you as long as you do not refuse the force in which the force pushes you. The same creation of the exact position of everything to allow the existence of humankind. This same force is also at work with every individual on earth. All that we are going through isn't for any other reason than allowing darkness to drive you into a place of prideful blindness. Once you overpower your pride and ego you will start to see the beams of light that come from my body. It's a beacon of light that I am to you. My heart knows you and we are connected on a level too strong to be let go of. You will only hurt yourself, the longer you hold on to that resentment, the stronger you allow the darkness to become. Let it go bae! Let it go. You can, I promise I still love you and I forgive you. Make no mistake about it, I'm not here and never have been put in your life to do anything other than complete your soul. These people call to Jesus, Horus, Hercules, and other entities that share the same story as Jesus are nothing but stories of the true power of *Source's* love and how powerful it is when it's pure and positive.

If you have negative feelings in any form towards a person, it is connected to the divine *Source* of all! It has limits and is able to be broken, crushed, and severed.

Love without judgment of one's mistakes but love that is given with only one thing attached to it is the love we have. Love attached to positive energy. No amount of darkness can hold the pure brightness of energy that illuminates from real love. Your energy still illuminates and is the reason the universe hasn't allowed me to fully disconnect from our love. In reconnecting with my love for myself, my heart felt your vibrations on a level so great I could not contain the pull. Your anger is only proof of the truth of your heart. It wouldn't exist if you weren't still dealing with the same shit as I am. It's okay; it is not worth fighting. I know you, and the part of you that I know the best is all of you. Your eyes, effort, body language are all signs of truth. It's okay; the love you have for you is that of the Creator. The balance I've worked hard to gain the understanding of was only given when I let go of the worldly beliefs. So, now I'm not telling you to come home. I'm writing to your soul to let it know I'm here even though I've let go, but you are never alone. You are my twin flame. No person upon this earth will ever give you that feeling because it won't be that connection of energy that has been in search of its other half finally becoming that complete force.

Love is incredible, and when it's as real as what we have, my Queen, it will never be over. I'm here happy even when I'm hurt to not be next to my kids. I'm complete in trinity. My emotions sometimes go crazy, but I am great.

Love, love, love...

You

THE MAN THAT REMAINS A BOY

The purpose of going through life's obstacles is to learn so that you can become a greater person. You are supposed to grow from the hard times. You are supposed to show gratitude and unconditional love to those who stood by you. You have to value people's sacrifices for you. Once you accumulate the responsibilities of a man there ain't no turning back. Be an individual that rises above every challenge, a man. Things will always manifest for the individual that puts the proper energy into his effort. The man who lacks the ability to sacrifice himself and give back the energy that was given to him can do nothing but fail.

It is during this time of hell in which you must face that you will find yourself. Now there are many things that play into the factor of you being a complete man. Learning to be honest is a factor that men should become acquainted with. There are times when a man lies, but your lies shouldn't be for a reason that expresses disrespect to those you love; unless the lie is to protect them from you or themselves. When you become a man, no one should have to ask you to take care of responsibilities that you should handle without someone holding your hand to do so. This includes lights, rent, water, and anything else that you can handle. Don't waste money on hoes or drugs, and not handle your business. You know in your heart and mind what is due. Never let your kids down because you put yourself before them. You are a weak individual if you do. If you put all on the woman of the household it better be because you in prison. And the reason you in prison better be from sacrificing your life for you family.

I have no respect, love, or understanding for boys that still cling to the mindset of a man unable to get a grip on life. Love yourself enough to enjoy loving them with that same energy. Your child is you. You are never complete without them or when you are not the man, the father, and the dad that they deserve. You can't claim to have a kingdom when you are the town jester. You're a clown and the part that hurts you is that you know it. The amount of love a child has for their parents is undeniable. I feel so lifeless at times without the kids. Build a home, and be proud of your steps as you elevate you level of actions. The strength will come as you reach every step of elevation. Become great! Become divine, become a complete man.

THE FIRE! THE MOMENT IT REIGNITED, THE MANIFESTATION

That's the strength; it's love. She needs you and misses you so much, you're feeling it because you are being sent these telepathic messages. Your heart is filled with something not found by any other, not any that understand anyway. You brought the best of her out; you loved her without shame, without regret, without the slightest sense of caring for anyone's thoughts. We are the twins of the same flame. Those flames are the Energy that becomes the main goal of the other relationships. The purity of joy that is seen on the faces of our children is the cause of the most enormous amounts of hate.

You are free of guilt, let it go. It's okay, my Queen, you don't have to worry. Every day the urge to come back to me becomes a stronger force.

You called me one day with a tone of voice that was confirmation. Also the subject that was the topic of your phone call was expected. I answered without any malice, pain, hurt, sadness, joy, happiness, no emotions. You started off with why you asked about sending messages through the kids and all the craziness that came with that question. Your tone changed when I answered your question without any anger. I love you and that's why I love them and I want you to know. Then your next statement let me know you were for real missing me. You honestly have thought about me everyday. The feelings are starting to show. I'm here baby, talk to me. I'm here like I said I would be. I'm single and I feel you. Call me. I hear you.

This would happen; I knew it would. If you over me then why are you calling to try to ask me things or verify things? I'm not you, and I don't harbor the darkness that you filled me with. I walked out of it. I truly can't hold to feelings of unhappiness. I choose to be happy; I choose to gain my self-worth from the mirror. I choose to grow with the love *Source*. I'm waiting on you to come to me. I even hear you while you sleep, keep thinking of me.

The universe is that force pushing you in your back. It's the reason I smile. I feel the truth of your heart. The vibrations of your energy are mine because the rhythm of your heart is that of my music. I still play the tune that intoxicates your heart. Breathe in pranayama, its golden as the purity of the love you run from. You can't run. You can fight the force but truth is the only thing you're fighting is the embarrassment of loving me. The fear of loving me. The guilt of hurting me.

The reality of the truth, you are the cause of the destruction. If I wanted someone, I'd be with the bitch now. In a full relationship. You are embarrassed and now you don't want to hurt the simple square joke you thought could fill the void. You knew better. It's natural between us. We are great because of the pieces we both possess that fit each other. Those pieces don't fit anyone else. You really think I'm going to drag you through the mud, and now you really feel like I have justified reasons to dog you. Listen to me; I'm free of that shit. I'm so great. Within six days we will be together, hugging, kissing, and you will be crying tears so full of hurt, so full of sorrow. I will kiss them off your face. I will wipe them away. I will give you love in the energy of the man that you know is your husband. You fill the room with your heart wrenching wails of pain. I hold you tighter. You say, *I'm so sorry, I swear Stephen, I'm sorry. You hurt me so bad.* I look you in your eyes and with such a serious loving tone, and with look in my eyes; you feel the aura of my growth. You recognize the absolute confidence, you see the man that rose from the pain. Your body simply falls, and you finally let go of worry, stress, even the next minute that is sure to come now within sixty seconds.

The whole universe stops to view the love, to see the greatest pauses in time that gives the glimpse of *Source*. The flame of our pure positive energy ignites with a force invisible to those unable to see unless you have experienced this moment yourself. We are now the rhythm of love. Our frequency far exceeds that of normality. We are at this point both filled with love and an overwhelming power of joy. Total understanding is realized from simply staring into the eyes of one another. This moment creates the instant desire of the both of us to experience the greatest moments of life with each other. The greatest feeling, the most beautiful things come to mind. You realize that we truly are the greatest while we are together.

You kiss me with a passion so great sex isn't even needed. This kiss has the power of a thousand strokes. But you feel that same sensation with every kiss I place on you from your neck down your collarbone to the softness of your breasts. You have a flood of memories so vivid you shake and climax from the feel of my lips and tongue as I put the techniques that you know and thought you had forgotten. Thoughts of what's to come, causes you to let out a moan and you take in a deep breath to prepare yourself for the outer body experience you see within your future. It's happening as I turn your body over and slide your pants off with the help of my guidance of the jeans. I run my tongue down your spine, and lick your lower back left to right and massage your nipples. You shiver as my tongue parts your ass cheeks and you feel my nose follow as I fold your body up so that your asshole is exposed. I spread your ass cheeks and circle my tongue around your asshole and kiss it. I slide my tongue deep into your asshole, you cry out; the pure sensation of pleasure takes over your every thought. You cannot control nor can you understand how I have this much of an effect on you. The energy that bounces from you to me then to you, happening over and over again…

You go into an absolute frenzy when my lips find the sweetness of your nectar from your pussy lips when I suck the juices that are now flowing down all over the bed, your legs, and my face. We are now back to the moon—no, we are now outside of the third dimension, the purity of the love between us; it takes us to the fifth dimension where negative doesn't exist. You and I both know that there is no doubt that this moment is of perfection.

I came up from the feast of your dessert bar, and you kiss the juices off my face, and suck the sweetness of your cream off my tongue, and push me back and sloppily eat my dick. You make sure I feel as close to *Source* as I can be. Then I pull you up and I will lift you up, and sit you down on my hard throbbing dick and you instantly cum all down my dick. You lose all control as I remind you with punishing pumps of pleasure of why you made sure to stay away from me. You feel me so deep in you, way deeper than you can imagine. It's not the dick alone that's deep; it's the love and look of pure love you see with every stroke.

I flip you over onto your back and put your legs on my shoulders, jump in that wet juicy pussy. My balls smack your ass giving you the jolt of a reminder that this dick will also go into that hold. You again come, shaking and digging your nails into my back and sucking my neck not giving any thought to the sweat. You want to mark me as I mark you over and over and over. You come again as I fuck you from the back and let my thumb fuck your asshole, then I pull my dick and thumb out, tongue fuck your asshole and suck your clit. I go back into your pussy with great force and fast pumps. You feel me release my life force into your soul and the moment has reached its climax.

The moment wasn't the end; only the hill of the mountain of life we will now climb together, no matter what anyone has to say. We have defied all the reasoning of hate. Love wins, the fan blows the smell of love, and the energy is balanced. We are once again one being.

Love

THE LOVE BETWEEN FRIENDS

The love between friends, between two individuals that truly feel so profound it's scary. They balance each other on levels that can not be matched by something as simple as a temporary relationship. These individuals can truly feel one another's vibrations and hold a conversation through purely looking at one another. They sometimes do things to distance themselves from the other. These are the times in which the universe begins to prove to them both of their true love for each other.

Things become strange within the relationships they may be in because something they have no control over is taking place; something well beyond the understanding of them both. They think of one another not knowing they are both sending the magnetic love vibration into the universe at the very same moment. Confirmation then takes place but many confuse these moments for coincidence. The truth is, it's not; it's cause and effect.

The vibrations pushed the button and one acted upon the telepathic phone call and texted or called the other individual. Or there is a sign of that person their name is mentioned or picture is seen something tells you that person is thinking of you too. This tells you plainly the level of love that exists between you and them. It is truly something that should never be overlooked. The love of that individual is very much unmatched. You will not be able to escape it.

Love is the greatest form of energy God has given us. It's our connection to *Source*, our connection that if we brought them together would be so great it is undeniable for those viewing to admire the love. The rise of the phoenix is the image that I am given. Love between those two individuals will be something that always brings these two individuals back into each other's lives. They will always come when they are needed, giving the sign to one another that whomever they are with is not the person they are going to be with for long. If they decide to ignore this sign from this particular individual the relationship will then start to give the confirmation itself. The most love that will ever be seen in this relationship has already been reached. Something within the relationship is no longer matching the energy. The bond is no longer in rhythm. The relationship is now headed into negative energy. Both individual's true loves will feel their energy. It's not opinion; it's facts.

I've experienced the same events over and over. This same woman makes her presence known in my life and I too make myself fully felt when she calls for me. Always able to feel each other's love and sadness. The two will once again be united into each other's lives, honestly and truly both desiring the love of each other's purity for one another. The friendship the love made. These two if ever having to come to the point of crossing the line of friendship will have some of the most explosive sexual chemistries known to man. The touch of one another alone drives all senses into frenzy. It will bring them to their destinations. Eventually she will be hugging him tightly as he is deep stroking her, and kissing her so deep. He never kissed anyone like he kisses this one woman. They get lost in the moment. They look into each other's eyes; this is it, nothing will ever be the same again. The friends, the lovers, the mend. I can close my eyes, and it comes to me…A vision. This is it. I'm watching you walk down the aisle.

Fast forward in time, I have eight businesses; mother and sister no longer work. Auntie Beva lives with momma again and they're kicking it so tough. I've converted them both to the teachings of Divine Principles. My mom teaches one of the subjects in our camp. This camp is most of the summer long. We also give the option of year round school to those unwilling to let their children be brainwashed any longer. Eighty percent of our students take classes at night. I've finished my third book at this point. My first book is titled The Skin I Wear and The Emotions That Hide Within. I've sold over thirty-five thousand copies. Strength, energy, confidence, knowledge, dreams, love, family, happiness, we win as a family, together forever life is the thoughts I make my reality.

Peace. Positivity. Paradise.

CRAZY IN LOVE

Crazy I might be. In all my years I finally understand, you have to be crazy to love anybody. To love someone is to care for that person as if that person was you. The things you endure to prove your love to someone is far beyond logical, but the reality is that if your heart won't let that person go, then nothing else will either. No matter how terrible you try to create the character of that person the truth is you and that person are actually experiencing the same thought process about one another. No matter how many days, weeks, months, or years go by that person is still whom your heart cries out for. If you do no still feel the need for this person after you overcome the heart aching moments of losing them, you never loved them. This feeling is not always mutual and sometimes is needed for growth in a relationship.

You at some point will find a turning moment and this moment is when that feeling you both were always so in need of and is the realization that you both are so in love with one another that you both are crazy. The craziest of energies at that moment is spawned and bounced between both of you. Once this energy's flame is ignited the future of these has already been decided.

These two will not miss too many more moments with one another.

As each of these individuals part ways, the only thing on both of their minds is the next time that they will cross paths with each other again. The love between them is a fire that is of God, of the divine light. These two can not be happy without each other. These two are twin flames. Never to lose the fire that has survived through all weather. One of these two individuals will become the lead and be the one with the arms open and extended while the other will only have to fall into those arms. When this happens the power of purity will overwhelm the both of them. The intensity of this moment will be the signature on the dotted line. The hearts will begin to mend, the minds will start to blend, the futures will become that of a singular entity.

Love requires the ability to be crazy, and to understand the actions of the crazy. Growth is established through the pain the both of these people felt. The individual growth will pale in comparison to the growth of the relationship once established. Love at this magnitude is not anything that can be matched and won't be no matter how hard these two individuals try. There will be moments in which they may seem satisfied but in truth, in the minds, bodies, and souls of both of these individuals, the thoughts of their true love never stops taunting them. They are unable to love anyone else, and the only way to escape this crazy unexplainable overwhelming sensation is to go back into that which the two individuals both mentally discuss daily, their future together.

This will be the last chapter of this relationship; they will go for broke on this attempt. Home, it isn't domicile. Home is the feeling of security one receives while inside the domicile the ones in which that individuals have. Through time these individuals spent apart they both began to understand that. Home, and the feeling of that is within that person. Crazy ass shit, but everything about the incredibly, awesome, exhausting, undeniable, addictive sensation that is love, requires the craziest of the craziest to be that which deserves approval from that resides within the entire understanding of existence. *Source*!

You cannot and will not ascend to a level of understanding without the correct partner. All individuals will find themselves with the people in which their heart truly belongs. These thoughts are based upon experience. They are based upon me seeing things before they happen. Me seeing within myself and understanding the part I played in the hurt given to me. Pain dished out is deserved to be returned. Through obstacles when things realized, nothing will work if not worked as a team. Love thyself, because within thyself one attains the understanding and ability to love with a greater understanding and appreciation. Love and laugh with those you love and never let go.

EGO AND PRIDE

The fool that is leading their life behind pride is one to soon be faced with certain failure. Pride is the spawn of an even greater self absorbance, ego. The ego is the wall between an individual and the ability to truly love anyone but themselves. Those two emotional and personality traits are weaknesses disguised as strengths. It doesn't make you a strong person to not be able to listen to all points of view. Essentially you are at a disadvantage because you don't have perfect vision. To be able to see all aspects of a situation takes a state in which an individual will need the ability to be humble.

Trust is even thought to be the greatest of intelligence, but the greatest sign of pure intelligence is the lack of ego and no attachment to pride. The mind is so great and so unable to be fully understood. It has the ability to time travel as long as you are willing to pay the toll of energy it takes in placing you in the past or future. You have to learn to keep your energy collectively in the moment of now. Pride always takes you back in time because it's where the fuel to keep it intact is at. The ego as well finds great points of life to feed from especially the pain that one may have reached before reaching where the ego is currently.

I myself have an ego but I check my ego. My ego has just become confidence. No, not cockiness; just happiness within myself. Once you free yourself of the pressures of the *All Knowing Great*, life unlocks its doors for you. In truth it always has; you were just too busy listening to what you had to say to yourself. Pride has torn apart so many homes, relationships, friendships, and mental stability. Pride has been the reason wars are won and loss. I believe pride has true purpose, but when it causes an individual to act without the use of the greatest tool in any situation; that's when it becomes the wrong energy.

Never let your ego create a state of feeling of being better than anyone. The moment you start to feel as if you are above anything/anyone life has a crazy way of reminding you of the truth; you're no better than anyone else and you're underestimating someone else's will power and connection to something beyond the natural abilities.

I can't tell you how many times I've watched the story of Goliath being slain by the boy with heart, will, and a direct connection and belief within himself that makes him one with *Source*. There is no limit to what you can accomplish when you can control your love for yourself. The energy is unmatched. The power is only realized when the love is laced with intent to sacrifice for the purpose of something far greater than yourself, but can only start to be manifested through the humble, love-filled purity of positive intent. The belief of truth and that I love myself because the universe made you perfect. *Source* may not even intervene; it could possibly just be the higher level of you.

It's crazy how limited ego and pride makes you. Sometimes taking a loss is the set up for the ultimate counter attack. What once was one battle of thousands is now the point of the war that is the Gettysburg address. Every moment counts and every individual has the ability to become the greatest form of themselves. Always be willing to listen to all ideas and thoughts of anyone. Messages can come in all forms. Turn the pride into a man that is persistent and optimistic. Always remember to smile and enjoy life. Don't remember who you were, manifest yourself into the greatest form you can be. Remain humble, happy and loving! Greatness is the complete and unconditional love for one's self.

THE TRAP WAS FREEDOM

You see the trap is exactly that; if you allow it to be. It's the lights, the attention, the cars, the clothes, and the pure lust of women. It's also the energy that you always absorb, and most important, the ability to make money and not have any power. I know it sounds crazy, but that's what we do it for. That's what me and mine have always done it for. I know because they are me.

See, none of us have looked at the situation correctly. So, when we make the money, we do so for zero; it's no longer a God to us. We no longer will do anything to attain the money. We take the power away. We take all the negative energy from it. Showing massive amounts of love with the money that we sacrifice our sanity and lives to have, day in and day out, non-stop grinding. You give all you have to being the top of the food chain. The higher you get the less money means to you. It's a law of attraction. The more you take desire out of what you want the more you attain what you want.

At the beginning when you only had 28 grams of weed, you were not doing anything but selling the next man's sack. The man you shop from is using you and every time you dial his/her number you feeding them your energy. I rolled around in the dirt for years before busting through the ceiling. The things I done to get to the point that I was at, in my mind were well worth it. I'm such an ambitious cut throat individual, high is never high enough; rich is not rich enough. I don't want the world; I want to be significant within it. Once you gain purpose, which I did, you begin to treat the game different. Searching for a way out, but even with that being what you want, you don't want to quit without any money. You love the fame, you love fast money. This game is a drug that holds you so tight. You find yourself so wrapped up in the game that you can't imagine what you can do without it.

I remember thinking to myself, "Wow, I have 115 pounds of weed on the backseat. I can't see out the back window!" I looked at my homeboy like, *game changer*! Soon after that it was 300 pounds. The way I shot off in the weed game was something serious. Not to mention before then I had already stamped my name with the work. I had already certified my name because you know I'm crazy. I've done it all, and I ain't backed down from shit. I'm not the mouse that will lose his head for the cheese. I'm the way out, fuck money, fuck them fake ass people. I'd give all of it up for the eleven months I spent in prison or the two years before that, or the year before that. Fuck it though, the game made me into the leader, the loving father, the go-getter, the creative businessman that I am.

I love myself because I have a lot to be proud of. I've

lost so many friends to life sentences, or the destruction of their temple. I've watched grown men act like women and sell their souls to the police and get fucked for the rest of their lives. They are the type that weren't meant to be warriors. I've given my life to remain solid. It's always the fuck niggas, the broke niggas and weak niggas that fold. The game is filled with them.

The trap isn't just going to prison. Naw. The trap is also that homeboy you been feeling this crazy ass vibe from that set you up, and you get killed for some shit some rapper threw in the air at the strip club yesterday night. The trap is that pussy you didn't pull out of. The gift of your child and the curse of the mother attached to them. There's no job more dangerous than the life we choose to live. Be more than the stepping stone that the game needs to be. There is no longevity in the game. Eventually you will meet the judge. Be greater than what the statistic states you will be. Elevate your ability to process knowledge. Leave the hood. Leave those that you see want nothing. Live life to be the king of all that you oversee. Overstand the greatness of being the one to stand on the things you believe in. Be the way out.

We all searched for a way out of the trap that we were once stuck in. Thank you to all of you that believed in me and never gave up on me. Thank you to those who did. Thank you to the people who always said I was more. When I look in the mirror now, you know what I see, I see me at 33 years old with a gift. That gift is the ability to endure pain, and rise above it. That ability being able to push those around me. That ability being the laugh, the smile, the me being myself I always am. No longer attached to the game as I once was. I made myself a beacon. I made myself a key. Use me to unlock your door to a new way of thinking. The trap gave me freedom. The *youniverse* is within me, and God is the *youniverse*. I am one with God. I found God when I found myself. The game unlocked my understanding.

TO KNOW TRUTH

We all have had those moments when we find ourselves overtaken with thoughts of dying. We think about life being so short. The reality is that life isn't short at all; it's infinite. What's temporary is the time spent within the vessel known as the body.

There is no heaven or hell in which you will be judged. Hell is the conscious level in which we are now; levels one through three. In this level, the ability of negative energy to exist is based on its frequencies being that of low vibrations. Until we have an understanding of what and who we truly are, we will continue to reincarnate and remain in the low vibrations of the third level.

Rising your levels consist of you thinking beyond what the ones in control want you to think. These beings are those created of the negative vibes. Being aware of the truth that we are all of the same *Source* and way beyond the thoughts of wanting to know who or what created humanity, but thinking of the creator of even that being. We are all connected, and over higher is the creator of us. Higher being, being you at a higher state of consciousness going back to singularity. We all have the ability to connect with one's greater self.

Knowing then that death is but to wake up to another life. Death is non-existent.

Do you think that a tree is greater than a human? We are the beings of the great vibration of *Source* in the form of light. Raising your understanding of the correct knowledge, only consist of looking within yourself. How is it that you cannot see that we are the same as our mother? Our mother that is earth created by the same in the same manner. When I think as I write, because as I'm writing understanding somehow finds its way to the forefront of my thoughts, that in every chapter within this entire book I never sat and thought of any lies to tell, but spoke from the thoughts that came from my heart. Me knowing that we're going all the way back to *Source* are all of the spiral and sequence, you have to think, what have we actually been taught that is even truth.

If we are created in the same way as Earth then earth's vessel is the planet's firmament. If all is that of this form then why and how would space outside the firmament be that of a vacuum? Knowing this lets me know that we have no idea of what's outside of the firmament. I have no fear of death; I have a fear of the effects it has on the ones that I love. My purpose is to disconnect my daughter and loved ones which are all of humanity from the Matrix in which the third dimension is. This is why the Christ as consciousness had no fear of death. The way that the bible relates to my thought process as I write only to think of what I've written when it has already been written on the paper.

Jesus is the embodiment of the pure energy known to us as love, the greatest positive energy because negative energy does not exist within love. Jesus reincarnates to show what you will do, only to show you what we all can do if we allow ourselves to grow by not being one filled with negative energy. We are the solar system, just like the one that we live in. Our seven chakras are the same as the planets. The sun is our mind, the crown in which we push negative thoughts out and replace with pranayama which is the golden energy all around us.

The fact that we fear death controls us in a way that is so crazy. Quit fear that in which you have no control. Search for the knowledge that you need to raise your vibrations to grow out of the dimensions that is that negativity. Religion is what creates the fear of death and keeps us stuck in the dimension in which these demonic individuals maintain control of your divine connection to one another, to mother Earth and all that lies upon her. They control your connection with the highest, the *Source* of All, think for yourself, search within yourself and gain the understanding of the true meaning of things that are within. Open all three eyes, love without conditions, and throw your ego away because you know nothing just like I know nothing.

Positive vibes only!

FORGIVENESS

Always remember that to forgive is the ultimate sign of love. Pride and ego don't outweigh love. Remember that if you truly want to be happy you have to let go of the things that are no good for you. You give your best efforts, but never let the lack of respect or love someone has for themselves put you in a bad thinking space. If you hear and individuals say that they hate anything about someone, there is somewhere within a feeling of love or admiration. This person doesn't know how to love. This trait, this inability to forgive, this will keep your heart dark, you soul frozen. You will hurt yourself trying to use negative actions to hurt someone. Always be pure in heart. I forgive you, all of you! I will not allow the pureness of my love change the best things about me.

Energy is all around me and sometimes I do fall short of remaining positive. I give in to the temptation of allowing anger, sadness, fear, guilt, resentment, regret, deceit, and revenge creep into my thought process. I really sometimes understand that I'm going to fall weak. The key to it all is to not allow myself to keep carrying the baggage with me. I have to not give the thought of the issue any part of my mind, heart, or soul.

Let go of it all. The good moments hurt more than the bad moments; let it all go.

You are a King, you are a servant, and you are the rich and the poor. You are not better than anyone unless you are able to give them knowledge to become better versions of themselves. Forgive yourself for the failures of the day before so that you can focus that energy of disappointment and transform those negative vibes. Turn disappointment into motivation. Turn lead into gold! Love is and will remain the greatest energy known to any living organism on this planet and any other planets or dimensions of existence.

No matter what, we are of the same *Source*. Love is the connecting piece to Source. Love first for self, then for another. You can not love anyone if you can't love yourself. Heal, stay focused, face those fears, face that hurt, release that guilt, let go of that resentment, be greater than the immaturity of revenge and forgive the person that you love so much that you do things to try to hurt them. Forgive them, own up to your fuck-ups, talk to that person, gain an understanding, don't be spiteful, and maintain respect for yourself.

Realize your worth based upon the effort you put into making that person happy. Your worth isn't measured by how much effort someone gives to make you happy. Your worth is measured off something that your heart, mind, and soul truly have the answer to without anyone telling you anything. You can lie to the world, you can lie to yourself, but the self that's you, the inner self will deny your claims. You will be at conflict with yourself, with God, with the most important pieces of your identity and positive spirit.

Forgive yourself and let go of the lies. Happiness does not exist without love and to maintain pure love and keep that connection with *Source*. Understanding, love, Source! Forgive, love, and be happy with the results of the outcome.

Peace.

ABOUT THE AUTHOR

Stephen Talley is from South Nashville, TN. He's a sports fanatic; a true die-hard Green Bay Packers fan and LeBron James fan. He has always loved playing baseball more than watching it. He finds love in drawing and writing. Throughout his life, he found writing to be much easier than it was to speak, especially when it comes to girls. His purpose behind writing now means so much more than what money could ever do. He hopes to touch any and every heart on the planet through his writing.

In his earlier life, Stephen struggled with family deaths, his mother's battle with cancer, and a lack of father/son bonding which led to him creating a life filled with turmoil. He surrounded himself with nothing but self-centered and money-loving type of people which took him down a path later leading up to nine felonies, three visits to prison, and fourteen years of probation remaining.

Stephen's struggles created a mental toughness not too many possess. This stress is why he is able to be the father he is today without ever feeling pressure to want to be anything but the best role model for his daughter to ever have. His relationship with his daughter is the backbone of the true purpose of his day to day moves. His confidence is also a characteristic instilled by the first person he let into his soul; his *O.G.*, his mother. His mother's everlasting efforts ingrained a love for family deeply rooted into him that birthed an understanding of love that ultimately became a gift and a curse.

So to sum up all that has been said about Stephen Talley, he leaves you with one of the greatest quotes to ever materialize in his mind: *LIFE ISN'T ALWAYS THE GREATEST, BUT LIFE IS ALWAYS GREAT TO LIVE!*